New Guinea Art in the collection of the Museum of Primitive Art

THE MUSEUM OF PRIMITIVE ART HANDBOOKS NUMBER TWO

THE MUSEUM OF PRIMITIVE ART HANDBOOKS

New Guinea Art in the collection of the Museum of Primitive Art

by Douglas Newton

The Museum of Primitive Art, New York   Distributed by the New York Graphic Society
Greenwich, Connecticut 1967

Copyright © 1967
The Museum of Primitive Art
15 West 54 Street
New York 10019
Library of Congress Card Number: 67-23358

Printed in the United States of America
by Publishers Printing-Admiral Press
New York
Photographs by John T. Hill 2, 3, 12, 14, 17, 19,
            21, 22, 53, 54, 70, 75, 76, 77, 85, 86, 90, 116
Eliot Elisofon 120
Raymond Wielgus 50
all others by Charles Uht
Jacket by Hiram Ash
Maps by Museum Planning Inc.

Introduction

I

New Guinea, an island comprising 317,000 square miles of swamp, savannah and mountains, is inhabited by about 2,700,000 people. They speak well over 700 languages which, although many belong to a limited number of families, are nevertheless for practical purposes quite distinct. Of these people at least one-third—generally those of the great highland areas—have in recent times practised virtually no visual arts beyond that of fantastically elaborate personal ornamentation. But the others, the people of the coasts and some of the inland rivers, have created a mass of sculpture and paintings with what sometimes seems bewildering energy and invention. Sporadically over the last half-century, and with increasing volume over the last decade, this sculpture and painting has poured out of the country in a flood which has now virtually come to an end. Many fascinating discoveries have been made in the last few years; but no large populations remain to be discovered, and it is unlikely that what small pockets of primitive cultures are left have any but the most rudimentary material equipment. By now the more important and artistically productive cultures are, to all intents and purposes, completely stripped of any objects of pre-European vintage, and have little or nothing left even of recent manufacture. We shall soon arrive at the point, then, at which we may consider that we have all we are ever likely to possess of indigenous New Guinea art before it fades out altogether. The future of visual art in New Guinea can only lie in the directions of folk craft, archaism, or participation in some western tradition.

If, however, we can strike a balance as far as the works themselves are concerned, we are in the embarrassing position of realizing that we know next to nothing about them. A great proportion of the extant material was collected in periods when communication between buyer and seller was not very feasible except in terms of the crudest transactions, and it must be confessed that skilled enquirers have not done a great deal better. Throughout a period when the functionalist school of anthropology was paramount, with its conception of society as system of inter-related, interacting parts, it seems to have occurred to few anthropologists that one of those parts was, precisely, art. Where art was not taken as a mere offshoot of primitive technology, it was as if they had taken seriously the contemporary doctrines summed up in the phrase "art for art's sake," and used its most superficial interpretation as a guide to the position of art in primitive societies. Some anthropologists even fell back on reporting that the only explanations they could obtain were that "the ancestors had always done things this way"—the first refuge of a lazy informant. It is only recently that programmes of research into the social aspects of art in New Guinea have been planned and executed; enough material has been published to indicate the wealth of the results, how impoverished our understanding of the art has been until now, and how much information is probably irretrievably lost. Only too often we are reduced to assigning works to categories of our own choosing which may have little to do with those consciously intended by their makers and users, who draw distinctions of which we are not even aware. The notes on the objects illustrated in this book are intended as accurate reports on the present state of our knowledge. I would be the first to admit, however regretfully, that they cannot be more than fragmentary hints of ideas, beliefs, and societies which in some cases have themselves been misconstrued by those reporting them.

II

The history of art in New Guinea is still a matter for speculation. The populating groups have been classified by the linguistic and ethnic characteristics apparently introduced by migrations, the most effective of which are thought to have been those of the pre-Austronesians about 3500-2000 B.C.; and the Austronesians, about 1500-700 B.C. It is presumed that these groups of migrants, coming from southeast Asia, not only populated the island but brought with them styles traces of which survive to this day. Accordingly some designs have been attributed origins in the late Bronze-Iron Age culture ("Dongson") of Southeast Asia. A few examples of Dongson bronze-work have been found at Lake Sentani and in the Vogelkop area, but the dates of their importation might have been considerably later than those of their manufacture, indeed quite unrelated to them.

It seems likely that parts of New Guinea share some elements which already existed in the early culture of Indonesia, but the items in the inventory of Dongson designs which are found in New Guinea are very few. The most important is the continuous scroll, which occurs in modified forms in Lake Sentani reliefs; much more directly in the various parts of the Sepik District; and in the Massim area. The process by which it achieved this geographical range is no more certain than the dates involved; granting that distribution was involved, it may well have been extremely sporadic and discontinuous. Perhaps more remarkable than any consideration of possible survivals from a remote past is the number of styles known to have existed over the last one and a half centuries. Ultimately these must be due to a complex history of major immigrations to which our present information gives us insufficient clues; even more to the effects of constant minor shifts of population and broken or renewed contacts between them.

The 700 languages of New Guinea are an indication of the peoples' diversity. The diversity is reflected in their art styles, but this is not to say that the most acute critic could discern as many art styles as there are languages, or even that language and style are topographically equivalent. All the same, while the number of styles which really existed at any moment one might choose to take as a cut-off point may be beyond computing, it must certainly have been an imposing one. Some of the factors working towards this variety, or acting as checks upon it, are worth considering.

In favor of variety, it is useful to remember that while any one group worked to a set of norms, which it quite simply considered better than any other set, in no sense was there—as has been asserted—a conception of supernatural sanctions which made departure from strict models dangerous or even censurable. Indeed it is hard to imagine how, among such determined individualists, such sanctions could have had any real force, even if they existed. It is likely that real adherence to established models was entailed mainly when, as sometimes happened, a new replacement was made for an old, valued object which had deteriorated. A tendency towards a fairly closely unified style in an artistically prolific society might exist when, as among the Iatmul and Abelam, large scale paintings and sculptures are carried out by a number of assistants under the direction of a master-artist. But among groups such as the Washkuk, which were equally (if not even more) prolific, an individual carves a figure or paints a single panel, single-handed; consequently it is easy to see wide divergences in style—not merely proficiency—between the palettes and technical range of the artists. More than this, in such groups a single artist may change his style more than once in his lifetime.

In the groups producing only small quantities of carvings or paintings, it must be remembered that only a few artists may be involved, each of them carrying out a very small number of works in a lifetime. In cases when replacements were not quickly needed, a new group of objects may not have been made for a couple of generations.

It is occasionally asserted that widespread trade in objects, and their further distribution as the loot of raids, increases the difficulty of assigning examples to areas, or defining local styles. The problem can be given an exaggerated importance. In its most sweeping form, influence was exerted when one group assumed the culture of another in a wholesale manner. Several instances of this are reported from the Sepik area and the Papuan Gulf; as a rule one group claims to have re-settled another on better land and, usually, to have taught it a higher culture. There were certainly cases of this kind of patronage, in which the patronized group's culture was not altered at all. In the instances when a cultural change did take place, it seems to have been a thorough metamorphosis;

but, in the art, a few traces of the old style often remained as assimilated elements in the new style.

Various factors working against partial influence may be mentioned. While "foreign" cults were adopted, even across linguistic borders, they did not necessarily include significant carvings such as masks; in fact, as a general rule, masks and figures were by no means the central cult-objects: these were, more usually, various musical instruments or imported articles which might be purely utilitarian in origin. Trade in secular valuables—in particular, shell ornaments—was very widespread, but prototypes acquired from other groups were not extensively copied: part of their value lay precisely in their exotic quality. Trade in sculpture or other art objects existed in a minor degree only, as may be seen from the fact that while the trade routes for recognized valuables were very extensive, the known distribution of traded carvings is not coextensive with them. In a very few instances, carvings were used in ceremonial exchanges as gifts. Communities might commission large and important works, such as an occasional housepost or slitgong, from foreign experts, but in no case were such acquisitions made across major linguistic or cultural boundaries. Still less would cult-objects of established sanctity be acquired from group to group, for the simple reason that the potential acquirers would consider such objects spiritually dangerous enough to be physically lethal. This did not altogether apply within a cultural or linguistic group: sacred flutes, for example, might be taken as loot by people who themselves used them. On the whole, however, a successful raid on a village tended to end in the destruction of as much property as possible. In the Sepik district the most popular articles looted were hand-drums and small, personally owned slitgongs; the victors in canoe-fights took, if possible, the ornaments set in the prows. There was certainly an interest in oddities from other groups, and trading parties were apt to buy them from time to time; but this seems to have been no more profound in motive than souvenir-hunting.

As far as active influences were concerned, trade in dances and songs, sometimes with associated masks and ornaments, was fairly common in the Sepik area, where it still persists. There is no saying how long the life of any such a cycle was; probably it was not of great duration. But if it proved popular, clearly the costumes and masks would have to be replaced by locally made copies. It would be at this point that modifications would be made to the original model, and that the new version would itself become a feature of the local style. Hence, probably, the impression of incongruity which obtains within some important styles; almost one of the stratification of a number of original styles, now compounded into a unit. There is, therefore, a considerable impetus in many groups towards internal variation in style, but also a good deal of restriction on minor influences from without unless they can be modified to accord with internal norms. Consequently any one style, while capable of a good deal of flexibility, usually manages to maintain its integrity—or perhaps, rather, a range of integrities.

IV

By now a number of studies have established the borders of several style areas. The existence of sub-styles within them is already recognized, and it is to be expected that, in the future, these sub-styles will be defined with increasing exactitude. The illustrations in this book are arranged by style-areas, first running along the north coast from the northwest to the southeast; then through the Sepik district; southwards to the south coast, at the east end of the Papuan Gulf, then westwards to the point of departure.

The first area represented is *Geelvinck Bay* (1-3), at the far west of the island. With work showing distinct relationships to that of eastern Indonesia, it is furthest removed in style from the rest of New Guinea. Only a narrow neck of land separates the Bay from McCluer Gulf, where a similar style is found; this also shows traces of the Kamoro style to the southeast. The next area to the east is the Sarmi coast (4). Further to the east, the architectural sculpture from the inland *Lake Sentani* (5-8) constitutes a strictly local style and is quite possibly the work of a limited number of artists over a short period.

The eastwards stretch of coast is the shoreline of the wedge-shaped Sepik district, and must be considered as part of it. Consequently the next objects illustrated are from beyond the Sepik coastline, the *Astrolabe Bay* area (9-10), with its stylistic relationships to southwest New Britain and some connections with the *Huon Gulf* (11-12).

A long coastal and mountain area follows, mainly unproductive of any visual art, until the *Massim* area is reached at the southeast end of the island, with its highly unified style (13-18).

The huge area drained by the Sepik River and its tributaries lies between ranges of hills to the north and south. In the northern range lives the large group of *Abelam* (23-26), represented here by works from their northern and southern divisions. Their styles are distinct from those of their neighbours of the coast and the river. Southwest of the Abelam, near the upper Sepik itself, are the *Washkuk* with another very distinct style (19-22).

The coastal Sepik styles (many of which are not represented here) extend eastwards from just beyond Humboldt Bay to the mouth of the Sepik River. They culminate in a style found near the mouth of the Sepik River among the *Murik* people (27-32). It extends beyond the mouth of the Ramu River, and also to the first few villages of the lower Sepik itself. Following a course upriver, the large *Anggoram* language-group (33-43) have several distinct styles. Flowing into the Sepik River from the south, the Keram River is peopled by the *Kambot* whose work (44-46) has features in common with that of the Ramu

New Guinea

MAP I

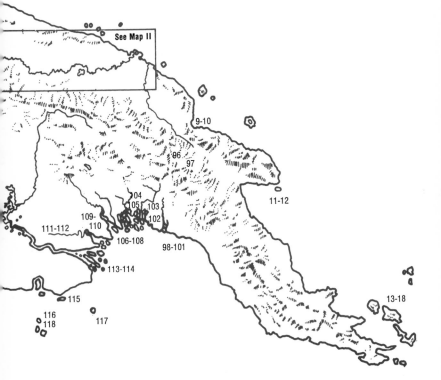

See Map II

9-10

96
97

11-12

104
105   103
109-   102
110
111-112   98-101
106-108

113-114

115   13-18

116
118   117

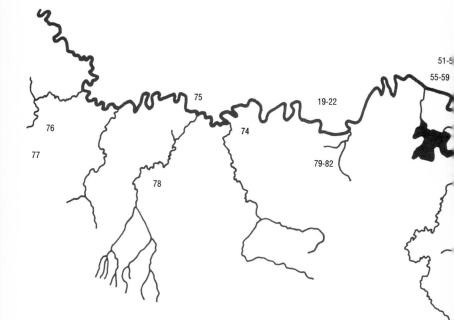

23-24

25-26

51-5

55-59

75

19-22

76

74

77

79-82

78

The Sepik District

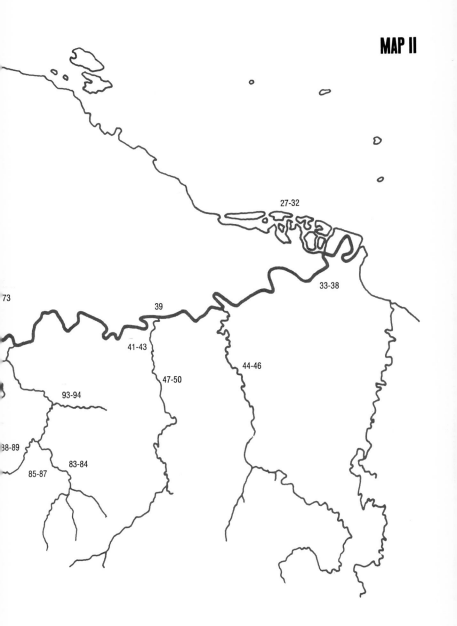

MAP II

27-32

73

33-38

39

41-43

44-46

47-50

93-94

38-89

83-84

85-87

River. The *Biwat* of the Yuat River (47-50) have styles related to those of the Anggoram, and even the Karawari River.

North of the middle Sepik River live the *Sawos* (51-54) with styles closely akin to those of the *Iatmul* (55-73) whose carvings and paintings have been well-known for many years, and are the most famous of the island. Their influence extends to the lower Krosmeri and Karawari Rivers (90-95).

By contrast the arts of the small upper Sepik communities, including the *Wogumas* (74), *Ngala* (75), *Iwam* (76), *"Awai"* (77), and the nomadic groups of the area (78), are sparse and impoverished. On the other hand, south of the Sepik there lies a huge stylistic area which, from the Hunstein Mountains (79-82) in the west extends to the upper Karawari and Krosmeri Rivers (83-89) in the east, with even some relationships to the Keram and Yuat Rivers (48).

In the Central Highlands range from which these southern tributaries rise, there lives more than a third of New Guinea's entire population. Although many groups have brought personal decoration, mainly in the form of head-dresses, to an extraordinary pitch of elaboration, they have produced extremely little carving in recorded times; the most interesting consists of the ritual boards of the Siane (96). The Highlands are also the source of most of the stone carvings (97) from New Guinea, though their origin is obscure.

Directly to the south lies the huge Papuan Gulf, with a number of tribes living along the coast. As an area this ranks only second in the sheer quantity of carvings produced (paintings are rare and negligible) to the Sepik district. It has been pointed out that there are very close coincidences in design elements, and even types of such objects as masks, between the Sepik and Papuan Gulf. However, fewer types of objects are made in the Gulf, and the number of distinguishable styles is not as great. The *Elema* (98-101) in the east form a large group with a style related to that of the *Namau* (102-103), the *Gope* (104-105) and the various groups included among the *Kerewa* (106-110) to the west. The *Gogodara* (111-112) live somewhat inland, on the Aramia River. At the far west of the Gulf, at the mouth of the Fly River are the *Kiwai* (113-114) a relatively unproductive group although the central Gulf was profoundly affected by their culture. They maintain ties with the islanders of the *Torres Straits* (115-118).

The trans-Fly region is inhabited by small tribes formerly preyed upon by the big Marind-anim and related groups further west still. For their ceremonies the Marind-anim construct huge emblematic costumes consisting largely of assemblages of feathers and light-wood carvings, worn by dancers impersonating various spirits.

To the west of the Marind-anim area again, in the swampy plain of the southwest New Guinea coast, live the *Asmat* (119-129), yet another group with a great output of carvings, though no paintings. Further up the coast are the *Kamoro* (130-132), who produce much the same range of objects as the Asmat. With this area the circuit of the island is completed.

The general notes on areas or groups are followed by references to the main works on them, which themselves usually contain fuller bibliographical listings. The notes on individual objects are followed by references to specific information about the type represented. No references are given for publications of the objects since their acquisition by the Museum, unless they are specifically discussed.

Native terms follow the description, in round brackets ( ). In the attributions of provenience, those made by the Museum are in square brackets [ ]; those without brackets are taken from reliable collection data.

The Northwest Coast

GEELVINCK BAY
Although divisible into several linguistic groups—including the Numfoor, and Waropen—the people living in pile-built villages along the shore-line of Geelvinck Bay and its islands shared a generally uniform culture. Alongside such common indigenous practices as headhunting and shamanism, clan-chiefs and slavery were less usual features of the social organization. These were probably due to Geelvinck Bay's relationship with the outlying islands of Indonesia: trade, particularly in bird-of-paradise plumes and slaves, existed between the Bay people and the Sultans of Tidore. Metal-working was practised by itinerant smiths from Biak Island, though on a small scale; no doubt the technique was introduced from Indonesia. Unquestionably the art style of tight scrollwork was influenced by east Indonesian models.
Held 1957; Gerbrands 1950-1951; Kooijman 1961; De Clerq and Schmeltz 1893.

1 Ancestral figure (fanderi). [Numfoor.] Wood, 7⅛" high. 58.210
These figures were made in a number of versions. The larger types (korvaar) either directly supported the skulls of important men or contained them in their hollowed-out heads; priests, entering into shamanistic trances, used them to obtain messages from the dead they represented. Smaller versions (such as this) were personal amulets. See *Kooijman 1961: 44-46; Gerbrands 1950-1951.*

2 Canoe prow decoration (bok). [Numfoor.] Wood, paint, 37½" high. 63.90
3 Canoe prow decoration. [Numfoor.] Wood, paint, cassowary feathers, 41½" long. 67.43. Gift of Mr. and Mrs. William J. Strawbridge, Jr.
A carving such as the horizontal example is attached to the end of a canoe prow, while one or more of the vertical type are set in a row down the length of it. The small human heads, in korvaar style, are pierced with holes originally fitted with plumes of cassowary feathers.

SARMI

The coastal people between Geelvinck Bay and Humboldt Bay have large, seaworthy canoes with outriggers; small carvings are attached at prow and stern. *De Clerq and Schmeltz 1893*

4 Canoe prow decoration (mani). Wood, paint, 11½" high. 67.40

LAKE SENTANI

Lake Sentani, seventeen miles long, lies surrounded by hills a few miles inland from Humboldt Bay. The 6,000 people lived in villages of pile-houses built out over the water. Considerable control was exercised by recognized chiefs (ondoforo), and their immediate followers, over economic activities (particularly trade with the people of Humboldt Bay), and over religion, which included a cult of flutes associated with mythical cassowaries. *Kooijman 1959; Wirz 1928.*

5, 6 Mother and child. Kabiterau. Wood, 36⅛" high. 56.225
7 Standing man. Wood, 34¾" high. 56.265
8 Double figure from housepost. Wood, 27¾" high. 56.244
The upper ends of posts, projecting above the flooring of jetties and the houses of chiefs, were carved with decorative figures, some of which probably represented ancestors. See *Kooijman 1959: 18-20*

The Northeast Coast

ASTROLABE BAY

The coast of Astrolabe Bay, to a depth of several miles inland, and the off-shore islands, was inhabited by a number of groups about whom little is known: the more spectacular aspects of the native culture were disrupted by about 1884, owing to the effects of colonisation. The main cult practiced by men was the *Asa*, for which special buildings were constructed in the bush to contain masks and other sacred objects. These houses were apparently distinct from the men's communal houses. Initiation ceremonies for boys took place only every ten or fifteen years, and then in the time between harvest and new cultivation. Their main feature was circumcision, rare in New Guinea, supposedly the work of a monster who devoured the boys but later returned them to life. *Bodrogi 1953; Bodrogi 1959*

9 Mask (asa-kate). Wood, 18⅛" high. 58.53
Masks representing spirits appeared in the dances and processions which formed part of the secret men's cult. In particular, it was a masked man who declared

the initiates mature at the end of the ceremonies. The circular projections on top of the head represent conus-shell rings, often worn as a part of a head-dress. See *Bodrogi 1959:55-59*

10 Male figure (telum). [Bogadjim]. Wood, 37¼" high. 56.92
In this area ancestral figures were often set up in front of the houses of important men. Some were displayed at feasts, when they were supposed to be the containers of ancestral spirits which were given offerings of food. In general they seem to have had a protective function. See *Bodrogi 1959:44-55*

THE HUON GULF
The cultures of the several language groups living around the coast of the Huon Gulf are dominated by the differing natural resources of their localities. Since none was self-sufficient, they developed a reliance on intensive trading in food and artifacts, carried as far as Astrolabe Bay and southwest New Britain in large sailing vessels. Among these were the bowls and headrests carved in Tami Island. Religious practices, including initiation, were virtually the same as those of Astrolabe Bay.
Bodrogi 1961

11 Headrest. Tami Island. Wood, paint, 4⅞" high. 59.92
Tami Island headrests were apparently only used as such in Tami itself. Elsewhere they seem to have had importance as personal possessions used in a funerary ceremony. This particular type, incorporating two human figures, was obsolete by about 1900. *See Bodrogi 1961: 91-79*
12 Bowl. Tami Island. Black palm wood, lime, 18¼" long. 67.2
This example is decorated with a human head wearing a three-plumed feather head-dress (oa-balan). See *Bodrogi 1961:99-104*

The Southeast Coast

THE MASSIM AREA
The people of the island groups off the southeast end of New Guinea are famous for the great trading cycle called the kula. Its stated purpose is to ensure the circulation over regular courses of two kinds of shell ornaments, possession of which brings considerable prestige. These are exchanged by trade partners who undertake planned expeditions in their sea-going canoes to do so. This ceremonial trading is accompanied by much distribution of other kinds of goods as in the Huon Gulf, certain localities specializing in definite artifacts.
Haddon 1894; Malinowski 1922; Newton 1967; Seligmann 1910.

13 Canoe prow ornament (taburi). [Suau]. Wood, paint, 42½" high. 56.84

14 Canoe prow finial ornament (munkuris). [Murua]. Wood, paint, 18⅝″ high. 66.26

Finials such as no. 14 were lashed to the tang rising from the top of decorative panels (such as no. 13) which were fastened along the projecting prows of the canoes. They were believed to provide magical assistance to the canoes' sailing. The lower part of the finial's design represents two reef herons; the dark areas of the carved forms above them represent nautilus shells embellished with stylized birds' heads. Stylized birds are also to be traced in the carvings of the taburi panel. See *Haddon and Hornell v. 2: 278; Seligmann 1909*

15 Canoe prow splash-board (rajim). Normanby Island, Bwebwaija. Wood, paint, 11¼″ high. 61.114 Collected by Géza Róheim about 1928. Gift of Dr. and Mrs. Warner Muensterberger.

A carving of a type fastened transversely across the prow of a canoe. At the top is a stylized figure of a child, with below it a double design representing breasts, or tattooing on breasts. The scrolls directly below these represent clouds at daybreak. Below again is an unturned crescent, with a central dot representing an eye. The design below this is a human belly, and the vertical bands on either side of it rainbows. These interpretations vary in individual cases; the lower part as a whole is often said to represent Matakapotaiataia, a great mythological hero. Illustrated *Seligman 1946: pl. F, 2*

16 Ceremonial axe. [Trobriand Islands]. Wood, stone, cane, 27⅜″ long. 59.27 Stone for the blades (benam) of such axes is quarried on Murua, and traded to Kiriwina, one of the Trobriand Islands, where it is polished and hafted. The carving of the haft (valela vaigua = "its handle is wealth") is also carried out in Kiriwina. The finished axes are prized items used for bride-price and gift exchanges. See *Seligmann 1910: 517-521*

17 Human figure [Trobriand Islands]. Wood, 4⅞″ high. 66.71 This squatting figure was probably originally part of the handle of a large lime-spatula.

18 Lime spatula (gabaiera). [Tagula]. Turtleshell, 11¼″ high. 57.87 Such outsize examples of this type of spatula are trimmed around the perforated edge with small discs of spondylus shell. They are carried by women in dances, and also form part of bride-price. See *Seligmann 1910: 516*

The Sepik District

THE WASHKUK

The Washkuk, living in the Peilungua Range and the swamps north of it, near the upper Sepik, consist of 2,500 people. Their chief cult relates to yams and their cultivation; membership of it comprises several grades. Only the members of the highest one—successful headhunters—are entitled to make the sacred

carvings which are revealed to the younger initiates. Nevertheless an exceptionally high proportion of men is able to carve, make bark paintings, and engrave designs on the clay of pottery bowls.
Whiting 1941

19 Figure. [Amarki]. Wood, paint, 54" high. 65.30
Such carvings were both sacred and kept in secrecy. The significance of this example is unknown, but among a neighbouring and related group of Yessan-Mayo, similar forms represent water-spirits, while the carved loops in the lower part represent a snake devouring a man. *Newton 1965*
20 Head. [Amarki]. Clay, paint, 15½" high. 65.43
Large pottery heads of this type were used as roof finials. See *Kelm v. 2, fig. 106*
21 Head. Clay, paint, 16" high. 66.48. Details of face on right restored.
Jars of this type are said to have been carried in dances. See *Kelm v. 2, figs. 17-18*
22 Painting. Tongwindjamp. Sago spathe, paint, 58" high. 67.60
Paintings are made in great numbers as ceiling decorations; the designs usually represent spirits of water and vegetation. This one, painted by Geipuk, represents flying foxes. See *Kelm v. 2, fig. 128*

THE ABELAM
The 28,000 Abelam, living on ridges of the foothills of the Prince Alexander Mountains, form not only one of the densest populations of New Guinea but one of the most artistically productive. The long cycle of ceremonies initiating men to the clan spirits involves the making of a wealth of carvings, basketry masks—the Abelam make no wooden ones—and the decoration of ceremonial-house facades with a mass of paintings and attached carvings. The clan spirits are patrons of the clan's pigs, and further the growth of yam crops.
Kaberry 1940-1941; Forge 1962, 1966

23 Ceremonial house facade decoration: hornbill. [Northern Abelam]. Wood, paint, 44¼" high. 63.7
Wooden hornbills of this type are attached to the lower parts of the facades of ceremonial houses. The design on the body represents the moon. See *Forge 1966: 30*
24 Helmet mask (baba). [Southern Abelam]. Basketry, paint, 16¼" high. 59.207
A type of mask associated with bush-spirits called wale, and used in early phases of the cycle of initiatory ceremonies. See *Forge 1965: 27*
25 Female figure [Southern Abelam]. Wood, paint, 42½" high. 62.158
A female figure probably of the type used by the Abelam in their initiation ceremonies. The initiates crawl between the legs into a narrow tunnel lined with paintings. The paint adhering to their bodies as they rub past it is supposed to contribute magically to their growth. See *Forge 1962: 16*
26 Ancestral figure. [Southern Abelam]. Wood, paint, 71¼" high. 62.81

THE MURIK

The Murik, about 1,000 people living in villages on coastal lagoons at the mouth of the Sepik River, developed an important trade system extending along the coast north-west of them, and to the villages of the lower Sepik River itself. In particular they specialized in the purchase from Manam Island of masked-dance and song cycles, which they then re-sold to the coastal and inland people. Their influence on the art styles of the whole area has therefore probably been very great.

Schmidt 1923-1924; 1926; 1933

27 Housepost. Mendam. Wood, 108″ high. 58.120
28 Carving. Wood, 44″ long. 59.255
Probably representing a group of ancestors and a totemic pig.
29 Mortar. Mendam. Wood, 3⅛″ high. 58.112
30 Mortar. Wood, 6″ high. 65.20
31 Mythological group. Wood, 9¾″ high. 57.79
32 Standing male figure (malita kandimbwag or murup). Wood, 7½″ high. 65.18

THE ANGGORAM

The people of the lower course of the Sepik River are culturally akin to both those of the middle Sepik River and the coast. Indeed it is probable that their ancestors came from both areas.

Reche 1913

33 Mask. Wood, paint, reed binding, raffia, beads. 18¾″ high. 56.65
34 Mask. Wood, paint, 15¼″ high. 60.53
35, 36, 37 Ancestral figure (konumb or atei). [Singrin]. Wood, 71″ high. 58.330
A memorial figure for an important ancestor, incorporating a number of totemic creatures. The torso itself is a silhouette of a crocodile, on which stands a figure of a pig in the round, this group being flanked by a pair of hornbills. Above the figure's head is a group consisting of a cat-fish and a woman.
38 Ancestral figure (konumb or atei). Singrin. Wood, 77¼″ high. 59.12
In this example, the totemic additions consist of an eagle on the body and, above the head, a stylized eagle (?) and hornbill. Illustrated *Reche 1913: 123-124; pl 19, 3.*
39, 40 Male figure. Moim. Wood, paint, 68″ high. 64.77
This figure of a clan-ancestor was damaged when the German colonial authorities, who administered the Sepik area up to 1914, shelled Moim village during a punitive expedition. Because the house in which it was kept caught fire, the figure was partly burned.

41 Shield. [Kanduanum]. Wood, paint, raffia, 65⅝″ high. 56.269

42 Mask (kandimbong). Kanduanum. Wood, paint, tusks, shells, feathers, fiber, 19¾″ high. 61.268

Like the long-nosed masks of the middle Sepik, those of the lower Sepik ideally appeared at ceremonies in groups of four which represented elder and younger brothers and elder and younger sisters. See *Haddon 1923; Newton 1965*

43 Figure. Wood, paint, 30½″ high. 58.79

Probably originally tied to a short length of bamboo and carried during dances. Illustrated *Chauvet: pl. 393*

THE KAMBOT

The Kambot language-speakers live on the Keram River, a southern tributary of the Sepik. They include several tribes, some at least refugees from the main river. Their ceremonial houses had semi-secret rear compartments in which sacred objects were kept, and were lavishly decorated with the bark-paintings which form an important element of Kambot art.
Thurnwald 1916

44 Mask. Wood, clay, shell, bone, basketry, human hair, cassowary feathers, 20″ high. 57.296

These miniature masks were attached to flutes midway in their length. They were used by both the Kambot and Biwat, who probably bought them from the people living in the swamp-land between the Keram and Yuat Rivers.

45 Painting. Sago spathe, bamboo, paint, 63¾″ high. 56.264

Paintings were used as decorations of the gables and ceilings of ceremonial houses, in a large area including the Keram and lower Ramu Rivers. This example shows a male and two female ancestors, and the heads of wattled or crested birds. The "X-ray" style of the torsos, displaying some of the internal organs, is most unusual. See *Speiser 1946*

46 Figure. Kambot. Wood, paint, fibre, 96″ high. 63.26

This unusually large figure originally formed part of a ceremonial-house post. The face is a double image in which the nose appears as a flute held by a lesser figure painted on the main figure's brow.

THE BIWAT

The Biwat-speaking people, living in a belt of land straddling the middle Yuat River, number almost 5,000; they are called Mindököma (Mundugumor) by their neighbours. In contrast to the main river groups communal religious life, the Biwat practised a number of minor cults, including those of particular

flutes, masks, and other objects, to which individuals held the right of introducing novices.
Mead 1935

47 Flute figure. Wood, human hair caked with mud, 21⅝" high. 56.70
A figure used as an ornament attached to the end of a sacred flute. Among the Mindököma these figures are called the "children of a crocodile spirit." The eyes formerly had shell inlay, and a beard or other ornament was attached by the holes under the chin. The great height of the forehead is intended to accommodate a quantity of shell ornaments swathed around it for occasions on which the flute was ceremonially displayed. Complete flutes were sacred family possessions, and were used as bride-price. See *Mead 1934: 238; Mead 1938: 200*
48 Ornament (manyan). Wood, paint, shell, fibre, cotton string, 15⅞" high. 57.6
A hair ornament for a large flute figure. *American Museum of Natural History 80-0.8328, 8331*. Stylistically related to the carvings of the Hunstein Mountains-Karawari River area (79-88). See *Forge 1960*
49 Belt ornament? Wood, paint, cowrie and abalone shell, feather, hair, fibre, 9⅝" high. 59.170
50 Mask. Wood, rattan, paint, feathers, 12⅛" high. 61.281

THE SAWOS

The 1,800 Sawos people live on slightly rising ground a few miles north of the middle Sepik River. While some features of their art styles may be related to those of the Abelam further north, as a whole their culture and art are very closely akin to those of the Iatmul on the river to the south. There is indeed a possibility that they are ancestral to the Iatmul.

51 Ancestral figure. [Western Sawos]. Wood, paint, fiber, 72" high. 59.202
Over life-size figures of ancestors were kept in ceremonial houses, tied to the posts. In this example the relief designs of crescents on the breasts and the snake on the torso probably represent scarification marks and are typical of Sawos figure sculpture.
52 Ceremonial board (malu). [Western Sawos]. Wood, 74½" high. 56.320
These panels are said to have been made to commemorate novices who died during the course of initiation, though this is far from certain. They were also traded to the Iatmul and Anggoram tribes. Illustrated *Newton 1963*
53 Mask (mei). Yamök: western Sawos. Wood, paint, shells, boars' tusks, cane, 23½" high. 65.44
54 Flute ornament. Kwoiwut: eastern Sawos. Wood, bamboo, cane, shell, paint, 62¾" high. 61.266
An exceptionally large example, the theme being that of the finials carved for

ceremonial houses: an enemy held in the grasp of an eagle which symbolizes the fighting strength of a village. See *Bateson 1965: 140*

THE IATMUL

With a population of about 8,000, the Iatmul are the largest group living along the Sepik River itself. Their sculpture and paintings, produced in great quantities, are the most famous works of art from New Guinea. Their ceremonial houses, the grandest of the island, were the focus of a rich ceremonial life including elaborate and prolonged initiatory practices, mortuary rites, and pageants enacting cosmic and ancestral myths. Headhunting formed a part of some large-scale ceremonies, as in the Papuan Gulf. All ceremonies involved the use of a wealth of masks and figures in wood or basketry. Besides such paraphernalia, almost all household objects are also decorated.
Reche 1913; Bateson 1931-1932; 1965

55 Debating stool. [Western Iatmul]. Wood, shell, paint, 31″ high. 63.52
All Iatmul ceremonial houses contained one or more objects of this type. During ceremonial debates the speakers struck the table-like projection behind the figure with bundles of leaves to mark their points. Although called stools (teket), these objects were never used as such. It seems possible that each was, rather, an ancestral image amalgamated with a stool which, with weapons and other daily objects, was considered its personal property.
The deep engraving (representing scarification) on the heavy pectorals, the undercut brows and the cross-ridge (a feather ornament?) on the head, are especially characteristic of western Iatmul figure carving. See *Söderström 1941; Muensterberger 1943*

56 Skull. Human skull, clay, paint, shells, hair, fur, fibre, 9¾″ high. 62.41
Skulls of both relatives and head hunting victims were stripped of flesh and overmodelled with a mixture of clay and oil into approximate portraits of the dead. They were decorated with the face-paint patterns used in life, and other ornaments. In this case, the forehead band of opossum fur indicates that the man portrayed was a successful headhunter.

57 Dance object. Yentshamanggua: western Iatmul. Wood, paint, raffia, fibre, feathers, 69″ long. 65.8
This carving, carried between two dancers in a pageant-ceremony, appears to relate to a legend about the origin of ceremonial houses in which the building is personified as a woman accompanied by two catfish. The fibre fringe may similarly refer to symbolic descriptions of the ceremonial house as a woman's fibre skirt.

58 Shield. [Western Iatmul]. Wood, paint, 54″ high. 56.322

59 Mask (mei). [Western Iatmul]. Wood, paint, shell, reed, 28⅛″ high. 57.253
Mei masks were worn for pageants enacted by younger men impersonating

pairs of ancestral brothers and their sisters. Ceremonies in which prisoners were killed by initiated boys were held under the leadership of a mei masquerader, who struck the first blow. It also seems that, on raids, mei were shaken towards the direction of the enemy to ensure invulnerability.

The mask was probably originally covered with shells, but has been stripped and repainted. The creature on the end of the nose is probably a frog. It is typical of the western Iatmul style of mei masks; narrow and with sharply undercut brows. See *Bateson 1965: 45, 233; Newton 1965*

60 Mask (mei). [Eastern Iatmul]. Wood, paint, shell, boar tusks, rattan. 23½" high. 65.44

Eastern Iatmul masks are markedly broader and flatter than those of the Sawos and western Iatmul.

61 Suspension hook. Eibom. Wood, 40⅞" high. 61.278. Collected by *La Korrigane* expedition 1934-1935

Baskets and net bags were hung on the prongs of wooden hooks suspended from the ceilings of houses, thus keeping the food and valuables they contained out of the reach of rats. Such hooks were often elaborately carved; in this case with a human head and the stylized head of a catfish. Illustrated *Rousseau 1951: 60*

62 Suspension hook. [Kararau: eastern Iatmul]. Wood, paint, 53¾" high. 61.280. Collected by *La Korrigane* expedition, 1934-1935

A stylized figure terminating in an eagle.

63 Woman and bird. [Kararau: eastern Iatmul]. Wood, paint, cowrie shells, 44⅝" high. 64.76

This carving, similar to those made as finials for ceremonial houses, illustrates a legend of an ancestral woman carried through the air by her sons, a pair of eagles. The woman's star-shaped eye-design within concentric circles is particularly characteristic of Kararau village. *Newton 1965*

64 Lime container [Eastern Iatmul]. Wood, bamboo, paint, reed, 22¼" high. 57.5

A container for the lime used in betel-chewing, a terminal ornament showing a rooster perched on a crocodile's head, made for presentation to an initiate by his mother's brother.

65, 66 Pair of slitgong beaters. Kangganamun: central Iatmul. Wood, 32" and 32¾" long. 66.49 a,b.

The carvings represent human heads held by hornbills.

67 Ritual object. Eastern Iatmul. Wood, paint, twine, 16½" high. 60.55

Several objects of this kind exist; it has been suggested that they relate to a mythical woman, Shotkamanagwi, who gave birth to a bird and a snake which made the channel of the Sepik River. See *Wirz 1955: 8-11*

68 Ceremonial fence element. [Kararau: Eastern Iatmul]. Wood, paint, shell, 60½" high 56.410

These carvings were incorporated into fences built around the sacred mounds at either end of ceremonial houses.

69 Neckrest. [Eastern Iatmul]. Wood, shell, hair, 24⅜" long. 61.275. Collected by *La Korrigane* expedition, 1934-1936

70 Female figure. [Eastern Iatmul]. Wood, 21¾" high. 61.276. Collected by *La Korrigane* expedition, 1934-1935

Such figures of women were pressed on boys necks during initiation ceremonies as part of their instruction to keep their heads down in fighting. See also the contrasting use of similar figures among the Abelam (no. 25). *Bateson n.d.*

71, 72, 73 Canoe prow. Wood, 71½" long. 55.1

The prows of most canoes of any size were carved as crocodile heads. Large communal canoes used for raiding by the Iatmul carried a group composed of a crocodile, a woman and a bird (broken off in this case) perhaps referring to the myth of Shotkamanagwi and the origin of the Sepik River (see no. 67).

THE NGALA

A small group of less than 150 people living in a single village, Swagap, until recently the Ngala lived in an isolation resulting from their reputation as ferocious fighters. Nevertheless their rare works of art often show, as in this instance, elements in common with those of their neighbours.

74 Canoe prow ornament (utukwei). Sago spathes, paint, wood, raffia, cane, 51" high. 66.6

For raiding expeditions Sepik River canoe prows were fitted with three-peaked screen-like ornaments made of sago spathes on a frame; wood masks attached to them represent clan ancestors. In this example, in a style unique to the Wogumas and Ngala, a projection above the mask carries a series of hooks and the head of a bush turkey or hornbill, representing a head ornament worn in dances. This example shows influences from the Iwam in the painted designs, and from Hunstein Mountains sacred objects (see 81-82) in the row of hooks. *Newton 1965*

THE WOGUMAS

The 400 Wogumas people live in four villages on the upper Sepik. They probably derive from the same ancestors as the Iatmul; however, little is known about their culture or language.

75 Canoe prow (kawt). Wood, 81" long, 66.5

The canoe prows of the upper Sepik River are as elaborately carved as those of the middle Sepik; those of the Wogumas tribe, however, represent not crocodiles, but a highly stylized hornbill with a row of other hornbills above it. *Newton 1965*

THE IWAM

Living in a number of small villages along the middle May River, a tributary of the upper Sepik, the Iwam (1,300 people) are cannibals with a simple culture and apparently little ceremonial life. Their art is confined to repetitive but highly ingenious combinations of stylized designs on barkpaintings shields, and a few utilitarian objects.

76 Painting. Sago spathe, paint, 52" high. 66.54

Paintings were used by the Iwam as door shutters and to line parts of their circular ceremonial houses. All the apparently abstract designs are symbolic; those appearing here represent opossum tails, human eyes, and crocodile claws. *Newton 1965*

THE "AWAI"

The small group of people living in hills above the May River are called Awai, or "enemy" by the Iwam, with whom they fight. It seems likely that they are immigrants from the direction of the Sepik headwaters, and related to the Mianmin tribe of the western Central Highlands.

77 Painting. Sago spathe, paint, 44¾" high. 66.36

One of a group of about fifty paintings found lining a deserted house. The designs are akin to those found on carved door boards of the mountain "-min" tribes (Oksapmin, Telefolmin, and others), and to those of the Green River north of the Sepik.

THE LEONHARD SCHULTZ RIVER

The Leonhard Schultz River area is inhabited only by a very small number of nomads, with linguistic and cultural affiliations to the Iwam.

78 Shield. Leonhard Schultz River. Wood, cane, paint, 67½" high. 65.46

The designs show a highly simplified version of those appearing on Iwam shields.

THE HUNSTEIN MOUNTAINS

South of the Sepik River, the Hunstein Mountains are sparsely inhabited by about ten small groups, none of which numbers more than about fifty. They built small permanent hamlets where their very scanty household and ritual equipment is stored while they undertake prolonged hunting expeditions.

79 Finial. Yigei-Yigei. Wood, paint, 30½" high. 65.95

Apparently related in style to heads of spirits carved by the Washkuk for their yam festivals.

80 Mask. Wood, paint, 33¼" high. 65.34
81 Cult hook (garra). Wood, paint, 49¼" high. 65.33
82 Cult hook (garra). Wood, paint, 36⅛" high. 65.32
The most sacred objects of the Hunstein Mountains tribes, these hook forms are from the western end of a style-area which extends across the southern Sepik district to the Karawari River. Probably representing stylized human faces (as is demonstrated by no. 80), they are regarded as the equivalent of sacred flutes (also called garra) and are apparently connected with ceremonials intended to increase the fertility of wild pigs. Like the flutes, they were concealed from women, but were carried by the men in dances. *Newton 1965*

THE UPPER KARAWARI AND KROSMERI RIVERS
The hills above the upper Karawari and Krosmeri Rivers are inhabited by groups which, in relatively recent times, have been influenced by Iatmul styles. However, they have also retained an older style, that of the now famous "hook figures". It is clearly related to that of the Hunstein Mountains, but has been carried in this area to a great degree of refinement.
Forge 1960; Haberland 1964
83 Figure (yipwon). Wood, 60¼" high. 65.38
84 Figure (yipwon). [Yimas] Wood, 56¼" 65.36
85 Figure. Inyai. Wood, paint, 46½" high. 67.45
86 Figure. Inyai. Wood, paint, 43" high. 67.46
87 Female figure. Inyai. Wood, 66¼" high. 65.40
These figures, in a distinctive style, come from the southernmost village on the Karawari River in which sculpture is found. See *Haberland 1964: 62*; illustrated, *Newton 1967a: fig. 2*

88 Figure (yipwon). [Karawari River]. Wood, 86" high. 65.37
These figures, kept in ceremonial houses, were considered spirits—or rather the media for spirits—which gave fortune in war and hunting, and whose intentions were interpreted by shamans. *Forge 1960; Haberland 1964*
89 Male figure. [Karawari River]. Wood, paint traces, 18½" high. 65.79
A naturalistic figure, the head of which shows a three-dimensional version of the two-dimensional head of no. 88.

THE LOWER KROSMERI AND KARAWARI RIVERS
The Kabriman of the Krosmeri River, the Karawari of the Karawari River, and the Kaninggara of the Blackwater River and Guvanamas Lake between them, are groups which—like those to their south—have been strongly influenced by the Iatmul, with whose art styles theirs are either very similar

or identical. There also are a few interesting strains of resemblance to styles of the Biwat and Kambot groups to the east.

90 Mask. [Blackwater River]. Cane, clay, feathers, 22¼" high. 63.8
Long-nosed basketry masks were frequently made in this area, as well as among the neighbouring Iatmul villages. This type, with a flat, broad nose, is relatively uncommon.

91 Mask [Krosmeri River: Kabriman]. Cane, tusks, feathers, paint, wood, bamboo, 67" high. 65.26
Huge basketry masks were placed in the gables of Krosmeri River ceremonial houses, as they were in those of the Iatmul. Many (including possibly this one) are still made in completely traditional style, for sale to Europeans.

92 Mask. Blackwater River, Terakei: Kaninggara. Wood, paint, shells, 13" high. 65.45
A mask with a clear relationship to the styles of the lower Sepik (see nos. 33, 46) and Keram River areas, rather than to the mei of the Iatmul.

93 Slit-gong lug. [Karawari River.] Wood, 35¾" long. 59.201
Karawari River slit-gongs have lugs, at either end, of exceptional size. The type shown here, with superposed heads, is also found in neighbouring Iatmul villages. The rounded noses, however, may relate to the Biwat style (see no. 50).

94, 95 Crocodile. Karawari River, Ambanoli: Karawari. Wood, paint, 25 feet long. 65.16
About fifteen huge crocodiles similar to this have been collected from the Karawari people. In function they are equivalent to the Yipwon, which they probably replaced under Iatmul influence: it is notable that groups of hooks form a prominent part of their decoration. See *Bühler 1961*

The Central Highlands

THE SIANE
The Siane (15,000 people) live in villages along the lower ridges of the eastern Highlands. Though they have a rich ceremonial life which is often carried out on a large scale—some occasions entail the gathering of thousands of people—their plastic arts are meagre. In this they are typical of the Highlands tribes, who largely confine their aesthetic output to the most elaborate personal ornamentation to be found in the whole of New Guinea.
Salisbury 1962, 1965

96 Board (gerua). Wood, paint, feathers, 55⅛" high. 60.88
These anthropomorphic boards embody symbols of the sun (the round head)

and moon (the diamond-shaped body). They are displayed in great numbers at large-scale ceremonies during which quantities of pigs are killed to feed ancestral spirits and promote pig fertility. See *Salisbury 1959*

THE PREHISTORIC HIGHLANDS

While cults involving stones used for magic and religious purposes are common in the Highlands and the Sepik District, stone sculptures are rare except in the central and eastern Highlands. These are generally very small in scale. Contemporary people have no knowledge of who made them or for what reason but, on finding them accidentally, smear them with fat and red ochre, and adopt them for modern fertility magic. None have so far been found in an archaeological context.
Bulmer, R. and S. 1962

97 Bird head. Stone, paint, traces, 4¼" high. 66.75
A number of stone bird figures have been discovered, usually representing eagles (?); this head, perhaps that of a wattled cassowary, appears to be unique. It may have been part of a pestle, though it has been suggested that such pieces were ornamental stoppers for sacred flutes akin to those found today among the Iatmul and other groups (compare no. 54).

The South Coast

THE ELEMA

The Elema consist of about twelve groups with a common culture, who migrated to their present homes on the eastern shore of the Papuan Gulf from the foothills of the central mountains. They are famous for the great ceremonial cycles, the most important being a cult of sea-spirits, for which they made colossal masks of barkcloth over cane frames, some being up to twenty feet high. The cycles took many years to complete. The celebration of the Kovave cult, of the bush-spirits, involved the initiation of young boys, who wore emblematic conical masks. The use of the rarer domed masks is uncertain. Like their western neighbours, the Elema made memorial slabs decorated with relief designs; wood sculpture in the round, however, is rare, as it is throughout the Gulf.
Holmes 1924; Newton 1961; Williams 1940

98 Helmet mask. Barkcloth, paint, cane, raffia, 37¾" high. 58.309. Collected by F. E. Williams.
99 Helmet mask (Kovave?). Barkcloth, bamboo, raffia, reed, 51¾" high. 58.94
100 Plaque (hohao). Wood, paint, 41⅜" high. 56.64

In this design the full-length figure is not shown; only the face appears with, below it, a circular form representing a turtleshell ornament. See *Williams 1940: 154-158; Brown 1954: 81-82*

101 Shield. Wood, paint, 32" high. 66.19

A small type of shield worn slung over the left shoulder to protect the left side from arrows.

THE NAMAU

Living in the swampy, flooded delta of the Purari River, the 10,000 Namau belong to four tribes. Their huge ceremonial houses contained big basketry animal-like figures embodying river-spirits. Cults of bull-roarers and masked ceremonies added to the richness of their religious lives. Cannibals, they culminated every important ceremony with the killing and eating of victims taken in raids on neighbouring tribes. *Holmes 1924; Newton 1961; Williams 1924; Wirz 1934*

102 Bullroarer. (imunu viki.) Wood, paint, 36" long. 59.140

Bullroarers are believed by the Namau to have great supernatural power, and are the focus of a special cult. Their name, meaning "weeping spirits", applies especially to the ceremonies in which they are played in mourning for important men.

103 Figure. Pie River: Ipiko. Wood, paint, 65⅞" high. 63.19

The Ipiko are a small tribe just northwest of the Namau and culturally very similar to them. As in other parts of the area, large wooden figures, singly or in pairs, are kept in their ceremonial houses. They represent Irivake, a mythical hero who is said to have invented headhunting. See *Wirz 1934: 100*

THE GOPE

The Gope are a small group living around Wapo Creek, between the Namau and the Kerewa. Their culture and art style have much in common with those of their neighbours, but show certain distinctive features. *Newton 1961; Wirz 1934*

104 Ancestral board (gope). Wood, paint, 50¾" high 62.82

The stylized figure on this board holds up its hands in what appears to be a formal gesture of protection, in accord with one of these objects' functions. The heart-shaped face is a characteristic element of the Wapo Creek art style.

105 Figure (bioma or agibe). Wood, paint, 22⅝" high. 62.86

These small figures are placed with legs in the eye-sockets of wild pig skulls, which are regarded as almost as important trophies as human heads. This grouping is unique to the Wapo Creek people. See *Wirz 1934: 76*

THE KEREWA

Emigrants from the Kiwai Island area have settled a large part of the Gulf to the east of the island, and helped to mould the distinctive Kerewa culture; this is shared more or less by about 25,000 people, some half of whom speak the Kerewa dialect of the Kiwai language. Their villages largely consist of enormous long-houses (flanked by small houses belonging to the women) which are also their ritual centres. Initiations, orgiastic fertility ceremonies and headhunting raids culminating in cannibal feasts, were carried out in a connected sequence which forms their most important religious activity.

Haddon 1919; Newton 1961; Wirz 1934

106 Ancestral board (gope). Goaribari Island. Wood, paint, 66½" high. 56.266 Collected by Bradley Patten, 1912.

107 Ancestral board (gope). Goaribari Island. Wood, paint, 64¾" high. 64.16 Collected by Bradley Patten, 1912.

These boards were owned by individuals, and each was named after an ancestor or a place. They were believed to perform a variety of functions, including warding off sickness and giving assistance in head-hunting.

108 Skull rack (agibe). Omati River, Paia'a. Wood, rattan, paint, 55⅞" high. 62.88

Most clans of the Kerewa settlements owned a pair of these half-length figures, one considered male, the other female. Skulls of ancestors and head-hunting victims were attached to the upright prongs. This is probably the largest extant example.

109 Ancestral board (gope). Turama River, Gibu. Wood, paint, 65¾" high. 61.113

An unusual ancestral board showing a stylized full-length figure. The spirals down the centre section are said to represent captured human heads.

110 Ancestor figure (kaiaimuru). Turama River, Gibu. Wood, paint, shell, 52" high. 61.111

One of the figures of men, women and animals tied to posts of the ceremonial house, and exhibited to novices on the last night of initiation ceremonies.

THE GOGODARA

The 7,000 Gogodara live around the Aramia River, in villages set on hillocks in a large swamp area. Each village consisted of a single huge house, some up to 500 feet long. With a culture similar to that of neighbouring groups, the Gogodara nevertheless had a distinct art style, notable for its use of abstract clan-emblems and rich polychrome.

Wirz 1934a

111 Canoe model. Aketa. Wood, paint, 45⅝" long. 60.92. Collected by Paul Wirz

The Gogodara laid great stress on the symbolic importance of their communal canoes. Full-scale models of such canoes (gi) were used during initiation ceremonies; this example is a small version of an initiatory canoe. The design painted on the side is the emblem (tao) of one of the Gogodara clans; the "prow" represents a totemic animal—pig or crocodile—holding a human head in its jaws. Illustrated *Wirz 1934a: pl. 47, 6*

112 Drum. Wood, paint, skin, 68⅛" long. 59.264

Only a single example of such outsized drums was owned by each clan of a village. Communally owned, it was kept stored in the roof, and only brought out for ceremonial occasions. The designs carved on the sides are clan-emblems.

THE KIWAI

The Kiwai people live on Kiwai and other islands at the mouth of the Fly River, and the adjacent sea-coast to the west. Like the Gogodara's their villages consist of long-houses of great size. They were great practitioners of magic devoted to increasing the fertility of crops and animals, as is their religious ritual. Their extremely sparse art is confined to a small quantity of figure sculpture in the round, and some decoration of objects used in magic or daily life.

Landtman 1927; Riley 1925

113 Dugong-hunting charm. Wood, 24⅜" long. 61.95

The coastal Kiwai (like the Torres Straits islanders) were enthusiastic hunters of dugongs, and dugong-hunting charms were kept in their boats. In general they took the form of sticks terminating in carved hawk heads. This highly elaborate example shows not only the hawk but the head of the dugong itself; the two are connected by bars which are possibly conventionalized bean plants. See *Haddon and others v. 5: 337-339*

114 Ancestral board (gope). Wood, paint, 32½" high. 61.64 Gift of Allan Frumkin.

Gope boards were semi-sacred objects with a protective magical function, and were placed as ornaments on canoe prows, or hung from house gables to ward off illness. See *Landtman 1933: 77*

The Torres Straits

The numerous small islands on the Torres Straits extend from close to the coast of New Guinea to close to Australia. They fall into several groups. The northernmost includes Saibai, while Erub is in the eastern, and Mabuiag in the middle western area. In spite of differences in languages and methods of subsistence, the islanders were fairly homogeneous in social organization. Cults commemorating ancestral heroes, and others designed to promote fertility

were practised, as well as important initiatory and mortuary rituals.
Fraser 1959; Haddon and others 1901-1935

115 Mask. [Saibai.] Wood, paint, string, 19⅞" high. 56.67
A mask worn for a ceremony (mawa) held about September to celebrate the harvest of ubar fruit. In most of the Torres Straits Islands only one man performed it. Wearing a voluminous costume of coconut leaves to conceal his identity, he walked about the village at night, chased men and women, and was free to take food from their houses. See *Haddon and others v. 5: 348-9; v. 4: 297-8*

116 Mask. [Mabuiag.] Turtleshell, clam shell, wood, cassowary feathers, seeds, paint. 25" wide. 67.48. Nose and right eye restored. Illustrated *Fraser 1959: pl. 13*

117 Mask. Erub. Turtleshell, human hair, 16⅛" high. 59.106
Turtleshell masks were made nowhere in New Guinea except the Torres Straits, where several types existed. They were worn for various ceremonies, including those to promote fertility. On Mer Island masks somewhat similar to this one were used in a section of the funerary ceremonies: five masked men, impersonating dugong fishers, mimed the rising and setting of the sun as a symbol of the course of the dead man's life. See *Haddon and others v. 6: 135;* illustrated *Fraser 1959: pl. 60*

118 Rain charm (doiom). Mabuiag. Stone, 5¼" high. 59.211
The doiom were invariably small stone male figures. They were invoked to send rain in various ceremonies carried out either by individual or groups of men. *See Haddon and others v. 6: 194-201*

The Southwest Coast

THE ASMAT
A vast swampland area of southwest New Guinea is inhabited by the 17,000 Asmat headhunters and cannibals. Their main ceremonies are performed for the initiation of boys; and to placate the spirits of ancestors, whose deaths were due to enemy action either in actual raids, or presumed magic. A great wealth of complex symbolism, much of it drawn from the natural world, relates to the taking of heads and the eating of human flesh. It finds expression in Asmat carvings, which are often on the grand scale, and their lavish decoration.
Gerbrands 1962, 1967; van Renselaar

119 Drum. Wood, lizard skin, fibre, shells, beads, 34⅞" high. 61.57
Drum handles are always decorated with ancestral and headhunting symbols, in this case particularly the heads of hornbills. The designs on the sides of the drum include "ghost-elbows" and stylized hands.

120 Masks: (above left) Ambisu; (above right) Pupis?; (below) Momogo? Wood, rattan, sennit, sago leaf, feathers, 65" to 80" high. MR140, P375, P356. Collected by Michael C. Rockefeller, 1961

The Asmat have no completely wooden masks; theirs are woven of string, with attached wood carvings, particularly eye-pieces. They are used in a ceremony by which spirits of the dead, after whom the masks were named, are expelled from the village. Some are also connected with the promotion of growth and fertility, of which the wooden tortoise on the lowest mask is a symbol. Illustrated *Gerbrands 1962, 1967*

121 Canoe prow. Wood, 32⅝" high. 61.58

A human figure with two hornbill heads above it. Illustrated *van Renselaar: pl. 29*

122 Canoe prow. Wood, 31½" high. 60.178. Gift of Dr. and Mrs. Warner Muensterberger.

Two human figures surrounded with stylized designs depicting parts of the body, and four hornbill heads.

123 Commemorative pole (bis). Etwa River, Otsjanep. Wood, paint, fibre, 15 ft. 6" high. Otsjanep 4. Collected by Michael C. Rockefeller, 1961.

124, 125 Commemorative pole (bis). Per. Wood, paint, 19 ft. high. UN 5. Collected by Michael C. Rockefeller, 1961.

These poles are highly stylized representations of canoes, the elaborate figures and wing-like projections at the top corresponding to an enormously exaggerated canoe-prow carving. The figures on these poles represent specific ancestors, whose spirits are ceremonially expelled from the village when the poles are erected. The ceremony is also a reminder to the survivors of their duty to avenge the deaths. Illustrated *Gerbrands 1967*

126 Mother and child. Lorentz River, Komor. Wood, paint, fibre, 55⅛" high. 61.52

The Asmat carve individual human figures for the inauguration of ceremonial houses. They represent wooden figures made by a mythological ancestor, who by beating his drum brought them to life to become the first people. Illustrated *van Renselaar: pll. 31-32*

127 Figure. Wood, paint, fiber, shell, human hair, bone, quill, 49½" high. 61.51

128 Shield. Lorentz River, Komor. Wood, paint, 51⅝" high. 61.59. Illustrated *van Renselaar: pl. 46*

129 Shield. Wood, paint, 57½" high. 61.60

THE KAMORO

The 8,600 Kamoro (or Mimika) live northwest of the Asmat, who formerly preyed on them in their raids. Though the two cultures were somewhat different—the Kamoro, for instance, were not cannibals—many aspects of Kamoro

art seem closely related to that of the Asmat.
Pouwer 1955

130 Mask. East Kamoro: Naikipiti. String, wood, paint, 10½" high. 61.174
These masks are worn by men impersonating the recently dead. They appear and dance on platforms set up for the purpose, afterwards being formally dismissed so that they will no longer haunt the village. See *Pouwer 1956: 386*
131 Canoe prow ornament. Wood, paint, 64½" high. 61.173
132 Bowl. Wood, 35⅜" long. 56.328

REFERENCES
American Museum of Natural History
n.d. Catalogue.

Bateson, Gregory
1931-32 Social structure of the Iatmul people of the Sepik River. Oceania, 2: 245-291, 401-453.

1965 Naven. Stanford.
n.d. Notes on artifacts in the Museum of the Faculty of Archaeology and Anthropology, University of Cambridge. Case guide.

Bodrogi, Tibor
1953 Some notes on the ethnography of New Guinea. *Acta Ethnologica,* vol. 3: 91-184.

1959 New Guinea style provinces *in* Opuscula ethnologia memoriae Ludovici Biro Sacra: 39-99.
1961 Art in northeast New Guinea. Budapest.

Bühler, Alfred
1961 Kultkrokodile vom Korewori (Sepik-Distrikt, Territorium Neuguinea). Zeitschrift für Ethnologie, 86: 183-207.

Bulmer, R. and S.
1962 Figurines and other stones of power among the Kyaka. . . . Journal of the Polynesian Society, 71: 192-208.

Chauvet, Stephen
1930 Les arts indigènes en Nouvelle-Guinée. Paris.

De Clerq, F. S. A. and J. D. E. Schmeltz
1893 Ethnographische beschrijving van de West- en Noordkust van Nederlandsch Nieuw-Guinea. Leiden.

Forge, J. Anthony W.
1960 Three Kamanggabi figures from the Arambak people . . . *in* Three regions of Melanesian art. The Museum of Primitive Art. New York.
1962 Paint—a magical substance. Palette, 9:9-16.

1966   Art and environment in the Sepik. Proceedings of the Royal Anthropological Institute: 23-31.

Fraser, Douglas
1959   Torres Straits sculpture. Ann Arbor.

Gerbrands, A. A.
1950-1951 Kunstijlen in West Nieuw-Guinea. Indonesië, 4:251-283.
1962   The art of the Asmat, New Guinea. Collected by Michael C. Rockefeller. The Museum of Primitive Art. New York.
1967   The Asmat of New Guinea. The Michael C. Rockefeller expeditions, 1961. The Museum of Primitive Art. New York.

Haberland, Eike
1964   Zum Problem der "Hakenfiguren" . . . Paideuma, 10: 52-70.

Haddon, A. C.
1894   The decorative art of British New Guinea. Dublin.
1919   The Agiba cult of the Kerewa culture. Man, 19, art. 99: 177-183.
1923   A new form of mask from the Sepik, Papua. Man. 23, art. 50: 81-82.

Haddon, A. C. and others
1901-1935   Reports of the Cambridge anthropological expedition to Torres Straits. Cambridge.

Held, G. J.
1957   The Papuas of Waropen. The Hague.

Kaberry, Phyllis M.
1940-41   The Abelam Tribe, Sepik District of New Guinea. A preliminary report. *Oceania,* 11: 233-258, 345-367.

Kelm, Heinz
1966   Kunst vom Sepik. Veröffentlichungen des Museums für Völkerkunde Berlin. Neue Folge ii. Abteilung Südsee vi. Berlin.

Kooijman, S.
1959   The art of Lake Sentani. The Museum of Primitive Art. New York.
1961   The art areas of western New Guinea *in* Three regions of primitive art. The Museum of Primitive Art. New York.

Landtman, Gunnar
1927   The Kiwai Papuans of British New Guinea. London.
1933   Ethnological collection from the Kiwai district of British New Guinea in the National Museum of Finland, Helsingfors (Helsinki) . Helsinki.

Mead, Margaret
1934   Tamberans and tumbuans in New Guinea. Natural History, 34: 234-246.
1935   Sex and temperament in three primitive societies. New York.
1938-49   The mountain Arapesh. Anthropological papers of the American Museum of Natural History. 36: 39-349; 37: 317-451; 40: 159-420; 41: 285-390.

Muensterburger, Warner

1943 On the sacred stools of the Sepik area. Internationales Archiv für Ethnographie, 43: 242.

Newton, Douglas
1961 Art styles of the Papuan Gulf. The Museum of Primitive Art. New York.
1963 Malu: openwork boards of the Tshuosh tribe. The Museum of Primitive Art. New York.
1965 Unpublished field notes.
1967 The art of the Massim area, New Guinea. The Museum of Primitive Art. New York.
1967a Oral traditions and art history in the Sepik district *in* Essays on the verbal and visual arts. Proceedings (1966) of the American Ethnological Society.

Pouwer, J.
1955 Enkele aspecten van de Mimika-Cultuur. The Hague.
1956 A masquerade in Mimika. Antiquity and survival, 5: 373-386.

Reche, Otto
1913 Der Kaiserin-Augusta-Fluss. Hamburgische wissenschaftliche Stiftung. Ergebnisse der Südsee Expedition 1908-1910. Hamburg.

Riley, E. Baxter
1925 Among Papuan headhunters. London.

Rousseau, Madeleine
1951 L'art océanienne. Sa presence. Paris.

Salisbury, R. F.
1959 A Trobriand Medusa? Man, art. 67: 50-51.
1962 From stone to steel. Melbourne.
1965 The Siane of the Eastern Highlands *in* Gods ghosts and men in Melanesia. Ed. by P. Lawrence and M. J. Megitt. Melbourne.

Schmidt, P. Joseph, S.V.D.
1923-24 1926 Die Ethnographie der Nor-Papua (Murik-Kaup-Karau) bei Dallmannhafen, Neu-Guinea. Anthropos, 18-19: 700-732; 21: 38-71.
1933 Neue Beitrage zur Ethnographie der Nor-Papua (Neuguinea). Anthropos, 28: 321-354, 663-682

Seligmann, C. G.
1909 A type of canoe ornament with magical significance from south-eastern British New Guinea. Man, 9, art. 16: 33-35.
1910 The Melanesians of British New Guinea. Cambridge.

Seligmann, C. G. and T. E. Dickson
1946 "Rajim" and "tabuya" of the d'Entrecasteaux group. Man, 46, art. 112: 129-134.

Söderström, Jan
1941 Die Figuhstühle vom Sepik-Fluss auf Neu-Guinea. Statens Etnografiska Museum. Stockholm.

Speiser, Felix

1946   Malereien aus Neuguinea in Museum für Völkerkunde, Basel. Phoebus, 1: 3-15.

Thurnwald, Richard

1916   Banaro society. Memoirs, American Anthropological Association, 3:251-391

Van Renselaar, H. C.

n.d.   Asmat art from southwest New Guinea. Amsterdam.

Whiting, John

1941   Becoming a Kwoma. Teaching and learning in a New Guinea tribe. New Haven.

Williams, F. E.

1924   The natives of the Purari Delta. Port Moresby. (Territory of Papua, Anthropology report, 5)

1940   Drama of Orokolo. The social and ceremonial life of the Elema. Oxford.

Wirz, Paul

1928   Beitrag zur Ethnologie der Sentanier. Leiden.

1934   Beitrage zur Ethnographie des Papua-Golfes, Britisch-Neuguinea. Leipzig.

1934a   Die Gemeinde der Gogodara. Leiden.

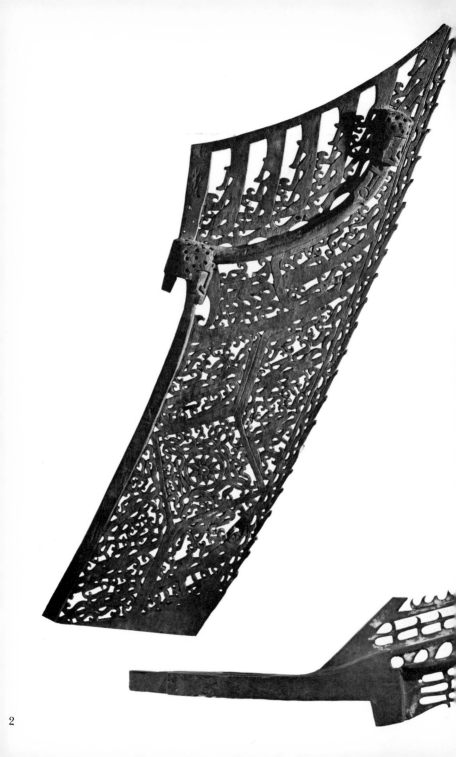

2

5

6

10

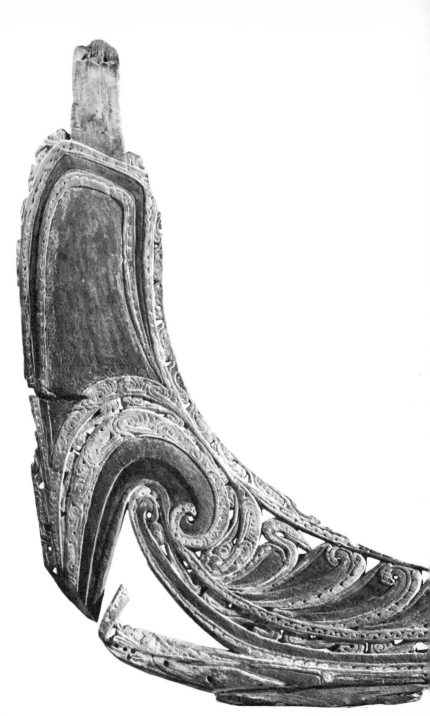

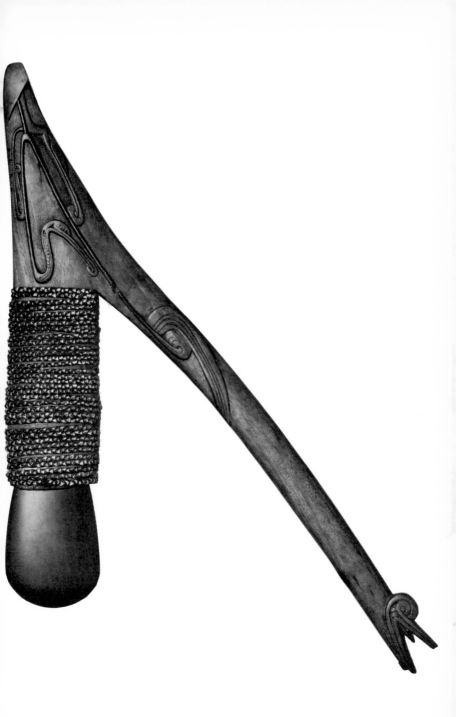

18

19

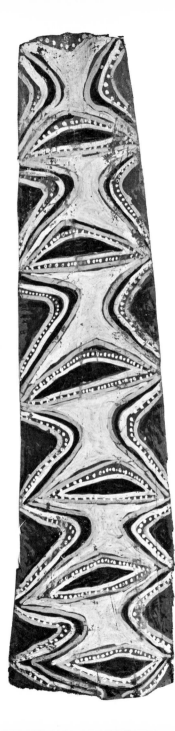

22

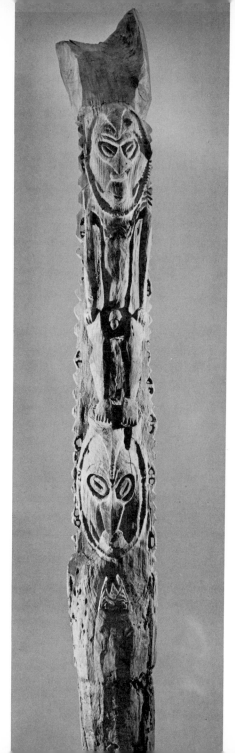

33

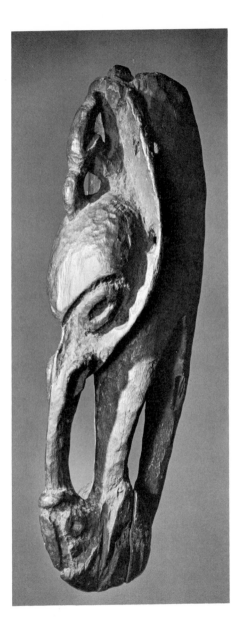

34

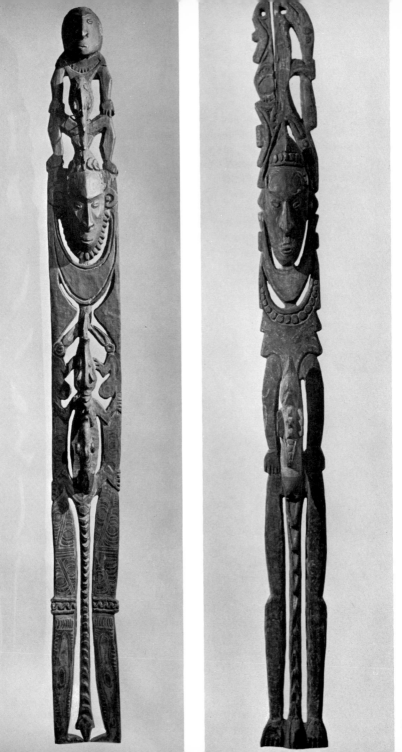

37   38

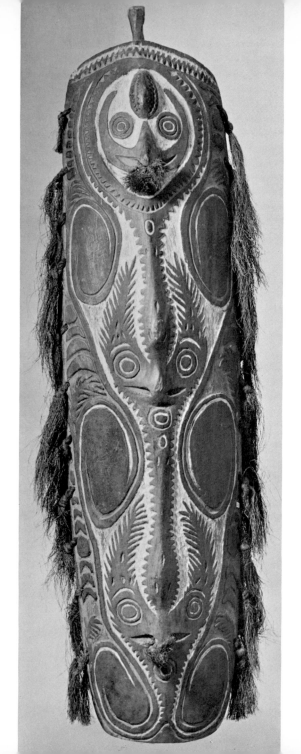

42

43

44

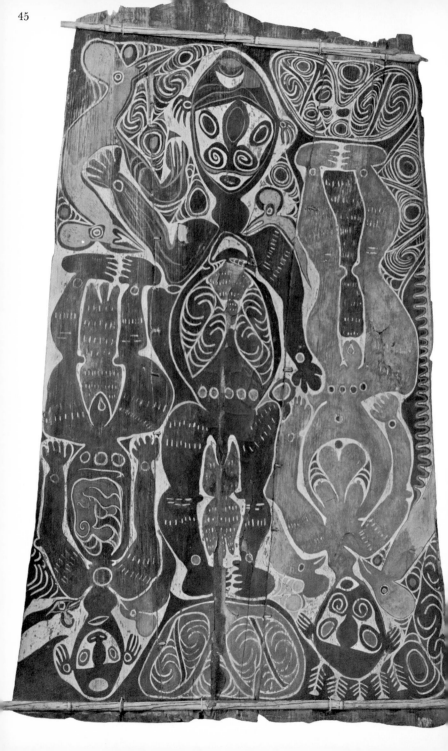

46

52

54

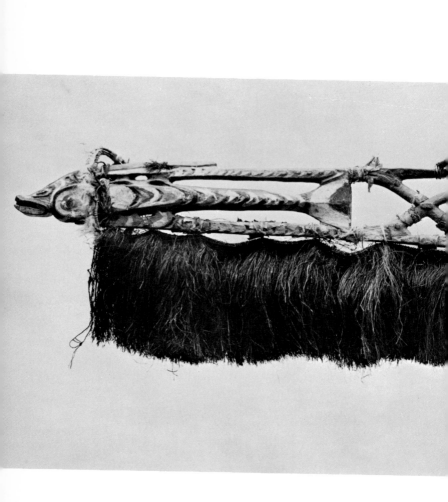

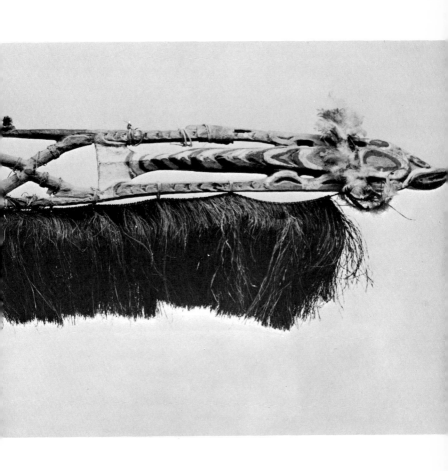

61   62

63

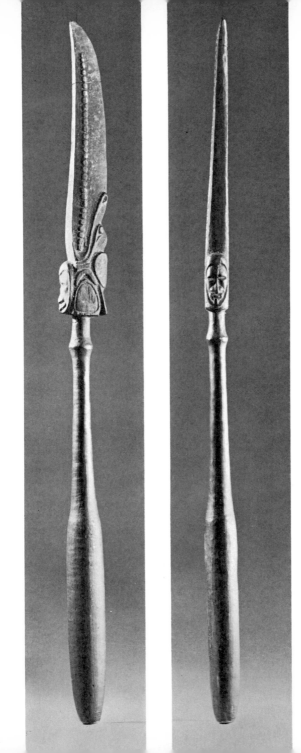

65, 66

69

74

76, 77

78

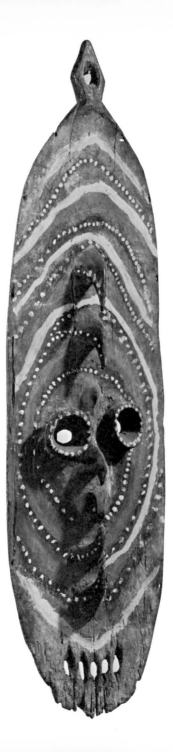

81, 82

85 86

90

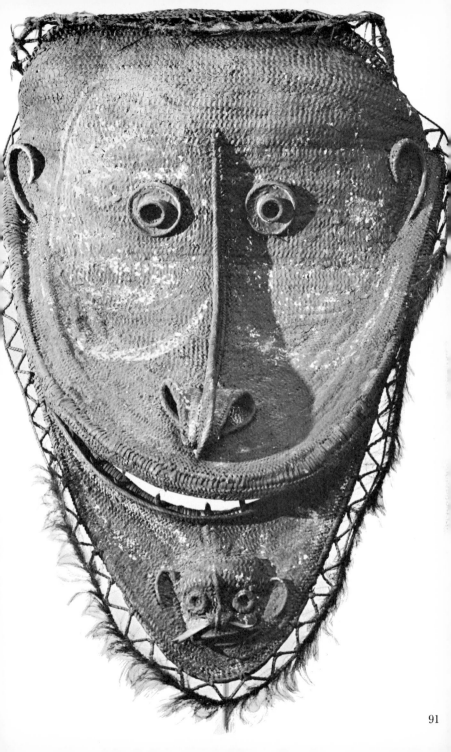

99

100

101

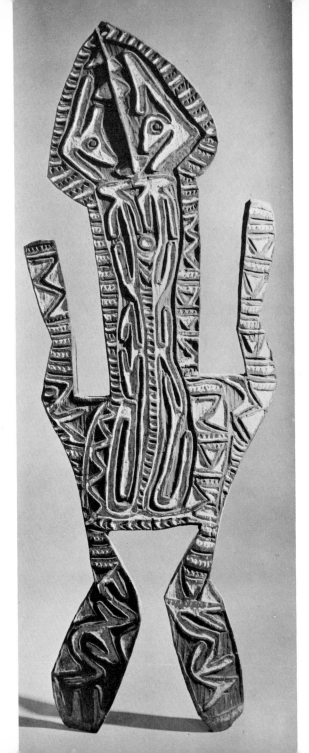

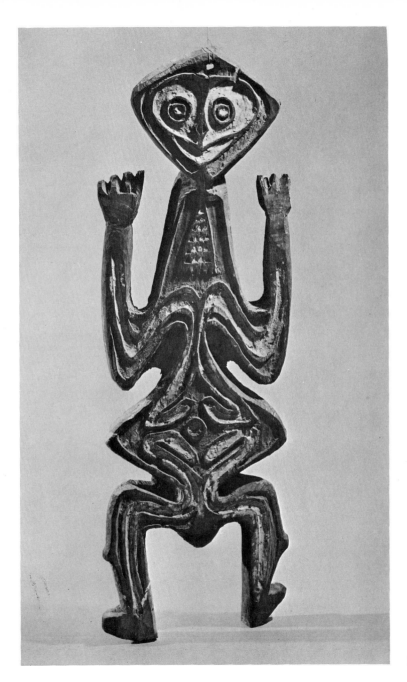

106   107

119

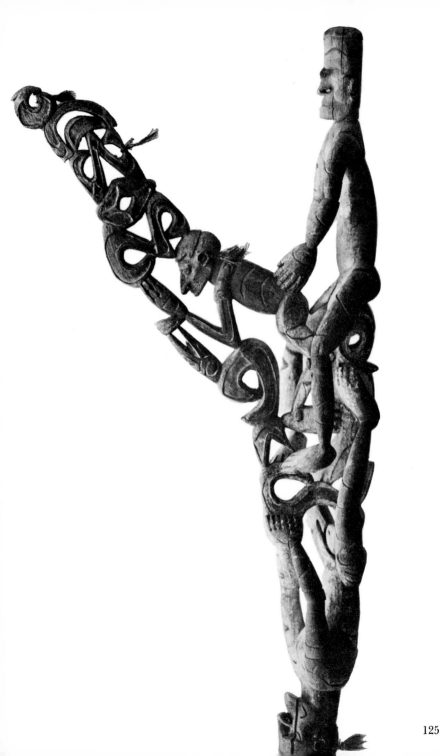

125